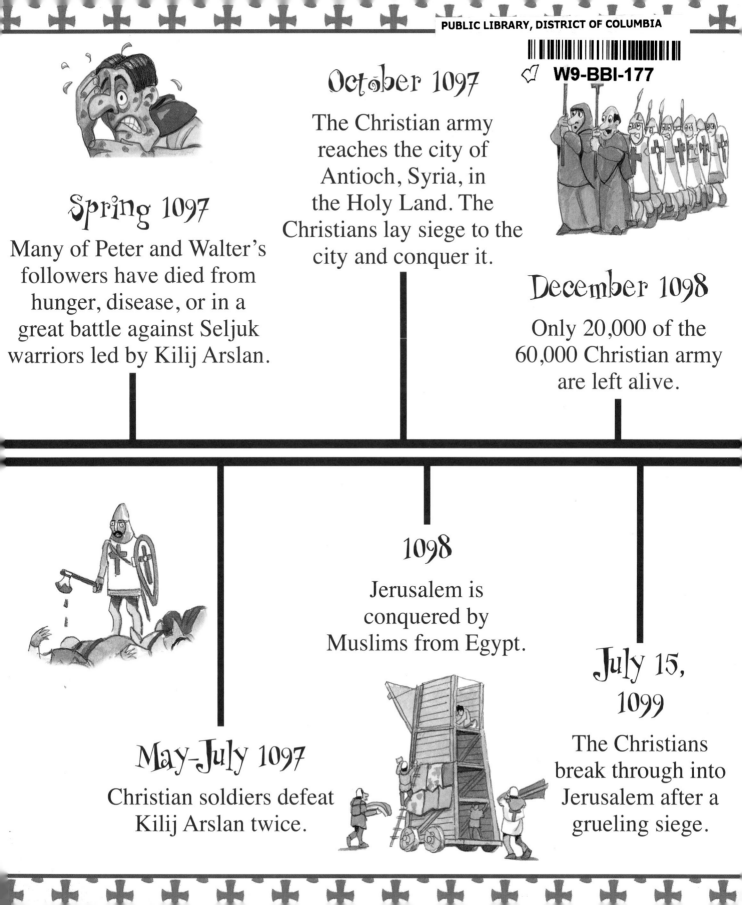

October 1097

The Christian army reaches the city of Antioch, Syria, in the Holy Land. The Christians lay siege to the city and conquer it.

Spring 1097

Many of Peter and Walter's followers have died from hunger, disease, or in a great battle against Seljuk warriors led by Kilij Arslan.

December 1098

Only 20,000 of the 60,000 Christian army are left alive.

1098

Jerusalem is conquered by Muslims from Egypt.

July 15, 1099

The Christians break through into Jerusalem after a grueling siege.

May–July 1097

Christian soldiers defeat Kilij Arslan twice.

Map of the Crusades

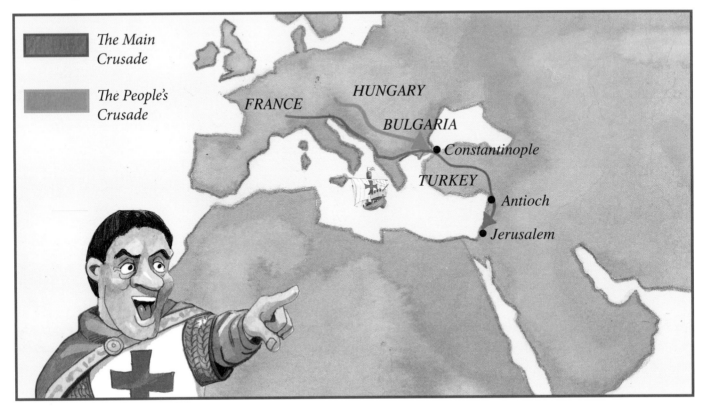

- The Main Crusade
- The People's Crusade

FRANCE

HUNGARY

BULGARIA

Constantinople

TURKEY

Antioch

Jerusalem

"The People's Crusade," the knights and peasants led by Peter the Hermit, set out across Europe for the Holy Land in 1096, causing unrest in Hungary and Bulgaria before they arrived in Constantinople (present-day Istanbul). Although some of the party crossed the river Bosphorus, Peter's army was attacked by the Turks and destroyed.

Meanwhile, the main crusading force, rallied by Pope Urban II, journeyed from France to Constantinople without any major disasters. From there, they swept across Turkey and into the eastern Mediterranean, laying siege to the cities of Antioch and Jerusalem. Once the lands of Palestine had been reclaimed for Christendom, most of the crusaders returned home.

Author:
Fiona Macdonald studied History at
Cambridge University and at the University of East
Anglia. She has taught in schools, adult education,
and college, and is the author of numerous books
for children on historical topics.

Artist:
Mark Bergin was born in Hastings, England,
in 1961. He studied at Eastbourne College of Art
and has specialized in historical reconstructions,
aviation, and maritime subjects since 1983.
He lives in Bexhill-on-Sea, England, with his wife
and three children.

Series Creator:
David Salariya was born in Dundee, Scotland.
He has illustrated a wide range of books and has
created and designed many new series for
publishers both in the UK and overseas. In 1989,
he established The Salariya Book Company.
He lives in Brighton, England, with his wife,
illustrator Shirley Willis, and their son, Jonathan.

Editor: **Karen Smith**

Assistant Editor: **Claire Andrews**

Consultant: **Dr Christopher Tyerman**,
College Lecturer, Faculty of Modern History,
University of Oxford

PAPER FROM
SUSTAINABLE
FORESTS

© The Salariya Book Company Ltd MMXVII
No part of this publication may be reproduced in whole or in
part, or stored in a retrieval system, or transmitted in any form or
by any means, electronic, mechanical, photocopying, recording,
or otherwise, without written permission of the publisher. For
information regarding permission, write to the copyright holder.

Published in Great Britain in 2017 by
The Salariya Book Company Ltd
25 Marlborough Place, Brighton BN1 1UB

ISBN-13: 978-0-531-23831-8 (lib. bdg.) 978-0-531-23153-1 (pbk.)

All rights reserved.
Published in 2017 in the United States
by Franklin Watts
An imprint of Scholastic Inc.

A CIP catalog record for this book is available
from the Library of Congress.

Printed and bound in China.
Printed on paper from sustainable sources.

1 2 3 4 5 6 7 8 9 10 R 26 25 24 23 22 21 20 19 18 17

SCHOLASTIC, FRANKLIN WATTS, and associated logos are
trademarks and/or registered trademarks of Scholastic Inc.

You Wouldn't Want to Be a Crusader!

I'm off to the Crusades, so I hope I'll be rewarded in heaven.

A War You'd Rather Not Fight

Written by
Fiona Macdonald

Illustrated by
Mark Bergin

Created and designed by
David Salariya

Franklin Watts®
An Imprint of Scholastic Inc.

Contents

Introduction

The year is AD 1096. The place, the kingdom of France. You're a dashing young knight from a proud old family. You've already won fame for fighting as a member of the army and in tournaments (fake battles) against your fellow knights. You are also a member of the army. You're not super-rich, but you own a small castle and some farmland. You have a family and trusty servants, plus horses, hawks, and hounds for hunting, which is your favorite sport. Do you really want to leave all this behind, travel across Europe, and risk your life fighting foreigners who follow a different faith? Read on and think very carefully. You might decide that you really wouldn't want to be a Crusader!

The Pope Preaches

Pope Urban II is a man with a mission! He is the leader of the Christian Church in western Europe and a forceful character who expects to be obeyed. For some time now he's had two great aims. He hopes to bring peace to war-torn Christian countries. He's also determined to defeat Turkish warriors in the Holy Land and to recover the ancient city of Jerusalem, over 2,000 miles away, in the Middle East. Last year, as you know, Pope Urban made a special journey all through France. Towards the end, he preached a rousing sermon.

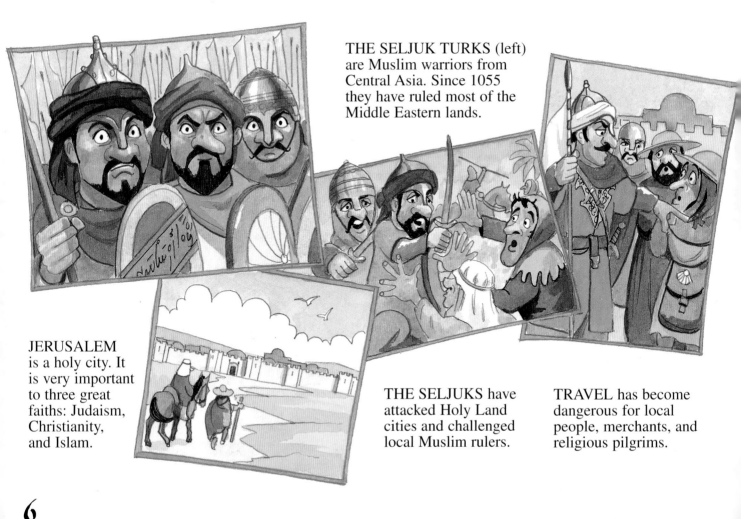

THE SELJUK TURKS (left) are Muslim warriors from Central Asia. Since 1055 they have ruled most of the Middle Eastern lands.

JERUSALEM is a holy city. It is very important to three great faiths: Judaism, Christianity, and Islam.

THE SELJUKS have attacked Holy Land cities and challenged local Muslim rulers.

TRAVEL has become dangerous for local people, merchants, and religious pilgrims.

WERE YOU THERE, with thousands of other Frenchmen, to listen to Pope Urban? His message was simple — and startling. "Stop fighting each other!" he commanded. "Start a Holy War against the Turks, instead!"

Handy Hint

Do your duty and fight! It's what the Pope commands!

Defend the Church! Save the Holy City!

What's So Special About Jerusalem?

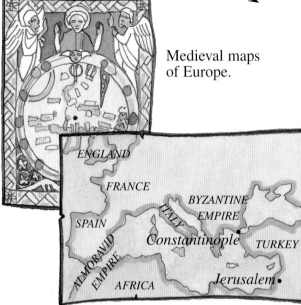

Medieval maps of Europe.

ENGLAND

FRANCE

SPAIN

ITALY

ALMORAVID EMPIRE

BYZANTINE EMPIRE

Constantinople

TURKEY

AFRICA

Jerusalem

MEDIEVAL MAPS (above) show Jerusalem as the center of the world. It's a favorite destination for Christian pilgrims. Over 10,000 visited the city from western Europe (map above) in 1065.

I n AD 638, Muslim armies took Jerusalem from the Christians. From AD 750 until recently, Jerusalem was governed by Muslim rulers based in Baghdad, Iraq. During most of this time, Muslim rulers allowed many Christian pilgrims to visit the Holy Sepulchre (Jesus Christ's tomb) in Jerusalem. But now the Holy Land is controlled by another group of Muslim invaders, the fierce Seljuk Turks. Pope Urban says they harrass Christians and damage Jerusalem's Christian holy sites. In 1071, the Seljuks also conquered a large part of the Byzantine Empire, a Christian state that rules eastern Europe and Turkey. Some people fear that, before long, the Seljuks might head west and conquer the rest of Europe, as well!

Holy Sites

MUSLIMS honor Jerusalem because it was the place where the Prophet Muhammad received a revelation of heaven.

JEWISH PEOPLE honor Jerusalem as the site of their holiest temple and as their traditional home.

AS A CHRISTIAN KNIGHT you honor Jerusalem because Jesus taught, died, and rose from the dead there.

MUSLIM CALIPH AL-HAKIM (above) was mentally ill. In 1009, he destroyed Jerusalem's Christian church on the site of Jesus's tomb.

TODAY IN 1096, Pope Urban claims that Seljuks are attacking Jerusalem's Christian churches.

We used to get 7,000 Christian pilgrims. Now, because of the war, none of them come!

Fight for God's Forgiveness

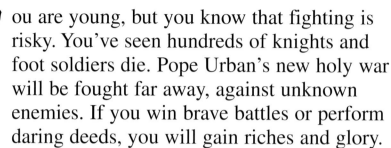

You are young, but you know that fighting is risky. You've seen hundreds of knights and foot soldiers die. Pope Urban's new holy war will be fought far away, against unknown enemies. If you win brave battles or perform daring deeds, you will gain riches and glory. But are they reward enough? The Pope has given another, better reason for joining his holy war. He has promised that God will forgive Christian soldiers' sins and reward them with a place in heaven. Going to fight may be a good way of showing that you're sorry for being sinful. It might also be a good way to escape God's punishment when you die!

GREED. Priests say that the love of money is the cause of all evil.

LUST. A great temptation to a lively young man!

ENVY. You want to have the best of everything, like your rich neighbors.

GLUTTONY. Eating too much is bad for your body and soul.

ANGER. Life is full of things that may annoy you, but try to control your temper.

SLOTH. Don't be lazy. Make an effort! Hard work might be good for you.

PRIDE. We all like to be praised, but don't let it make you big-headed.

10

Take Your Weapons and Armor

A PADDED CAP worn under your helmet adds comfort and protection.

It costs a lot to equip a knight for battle. Can you afford to join the holy war? A long heavy sword for slashing at enemies is essential, as is a sharp spear. You'll also need a mace (war club) for bashing them over the head and a dagger for stabbing. Don't leave home without your armor: a chain-mail tunic, a domed metal helmet, and a big kite-shaped shield — the most useful design when fighting on horseback. Spurs — sharp metal points fixed to the heels of your shoes — will make your horse gallop faster if you press them into his sides. They are a sign of high rank and only knights can wear them.

A LONG, HOODED, WOOL CLOAK will keep you warm in winter and at night.

A LONG SURCOAT worn over your armor helps keep you cool in desert sun.

BIG BREECHES, padded with cotton, protect private parts and prevent saddle-sores!

ONE WARHORSE is essential, two or three are better. You'll need baggage-horses too.

13

Preparing to Leave

You have almost made up your mind to obey the Pope's commands and fight. But you don't want to leave your wife and family. If only they could come with you! But that would be dangerous for the children. Like other medieval women, your wife is not trained to fight. Anyway, she has far too many duties to be able to leave home. Even now, she is in charge of running your castle, keeping accounts, managing servants, ordering provisions, educating the children, entertaining important visitors, and providing charity for poor peasants. While you're away, she will have to manage your farmland and will spend many hours praying for your safe return.

Before You Go:

GIVE A PEP TALK to your oldest son. Tell him to be good and to look after the family.

RAISE CASH! You'll need a lot for food and traveling. Some knights borrow money for this. If they don't pay it back, they will lose their land.

ISSUE ORDERS! You may be away for a year or more. Make sure your servants know what to do.

HAND OVER the castle keys to your wife. She'll take charge while you're away.

AT LONG LAST, YOU'VE DECIDED! You asked your wife for advice and she said "Go!" She thinks it is your duty, but she'll miss you terribly.

I might never see them again!

Handy Hint

Make a will! That way, you'll be sure that your sons will inherit your land.

Will You Follow a Hermit?

It is now April 1096 and you are faced with another difficult choice. Should you join the mob of ordinary people that has gathered together in Germany? It is led by two strange characters, Peter the Hermit (a holy man) and Walter Sans-Avoir (a French knight). They are setting off for the Holy Land right now! If you're wise, you will wait for a while and join an army led by an experienced military man.

> Follow me and find God!

Or Wait to Be Led by a Lord?

GODFREY OF BOUILLON is determined, handsome, courageous, and widely admired. His group includes his brothers Eustace and Baldwin.

BOHEMUND OF TARENTUM is a great warrior. He and the Byzantines have fought each other in the past.

RAYMOND OF TOULOUSE wants to be king of Jerusalem. He has his wife with him!

At ten miles a day, I reckon we'll be marching most of the year!

Handy Hint

Be nice to the Byzantines! They could be useful allies.

ALL WARRIOR LORDS have their faults, but at least they know how to organize a march, plan a battle, and lead a fight.

BISHOP ADHEMAR is a stern warrior. He wants to lead the Church in the Holy Land.

PRINCE HUGH of Vermandois is arrogant and foolish. He is also the brother of the King of France.

ROBERT OF NORMANDY is a pious man. He's borrowed money from his brother the King of England to pay for his journey.

Do You Know Where You're Going?

ou have no globe showing countries of the world and no maps either. In fact, there are very few maps available and most of them are pretty inaccurate anyway. You have heard travelers' tales from pilgrims who have made the long journey to Jerusalem. You have also met merchants who have sailed to trade at ports all around the Mediterranean Sea. But you yourself are not an experienced traveler. You have always ridden on horseback and have never been more than a hundred miles from home. You find it hard to believe that it might take months to travel from France to Jerusalem. And you have no idea of all the difficulties and dangers that lay in wait along the way!

A Dangerous Journey

LOOK OUT for puddles, deep ruts, loose stones, and potholes! All roads have them.

MIND THE MUD! In some places it's so deep that you and your horse will sink without a trace.

TAKE CARE on steep and narrow mountain paths! It's a long way to fall!

BANDITS AND ROBBERS lay in wait for travelers alongside many roads. They'll steal all your money and belongings, including your clothes, and leave you to die of cold.

YOUR FIRST TIME ON A SAILING SHIP. You'll discover it takes time to find your sea legs and stop being seasick!

Handy Hint

Take a good pair of boots! You'll be traveling over rough ground and doing a lot of walking!

Cheer up! The voyage only lasts six weeks!

MANY RIVERS have no bridges. You'll need to find a ferry-boat or swim!

STEPPING STONES can be very slippery! If you fall in you'll be soaked to the skin.

Your horse isn't able to walk across stepping stones. He might fall and break a leg.

IN WINTER, your route may be blocked by snowdrifts or covered in ice.

IN SUMMER, you'll suffer from the heat and dust, thirst and sunstroke!

19

Know Your Enemy

What do you know about your rivals, the Seljuk Turks, who have conquered the Holy Land? They have a reputation as fearsome fighters, but they are not savages. They have begun to join a multicultural civilization based in Central Asia. It combines ancient nomad traditions with ideas from Ancient Greece, Iran, and India, all blended together with the faith of Islam. The Seljuks speak Turkish, a Central Asian language, and dress in their own special style. They wear knee-length tunics and cloaks over baggy trousers and boots. The Seljuks have beards and mustaches and, sometimes, long, flowing hair. For battle, they put on armor made of little plates of metal and pointed metal helmets with turbans wrapped around.

The Seljuk Turks

THE SELJUKS are Muslims who follow the Sunni (majority) branch of Islam. They pray five times a day.

SELJUK SOLDIERS believe that they are fighting to help spread their faith to other, less enlightened people. They also want to conquer more land.

SELJUK CRAFTSMEN create beautiful rugs, silks, glassware, and pottery. The Seljuks build tall tombs of decorative brick.

IN BATTLE, Seljuks ride up close on fast, nimble ponies, shoot with bows and arrows, then gallop out of harm's way.

THE SELJUK COMMANDER is Sultan Kilij Arslan. He rules an empire based in Turkey. His army is recruited from two Turkish peoples, the Seljuks and the Danishmends.

Handy Hint

Copy the Turks and wear a surcoat over your armor. It will stop the sun from heating the metal.

Should we invade North Africa, Europe, or Arabia next?

Will You Be Cruel in Constantinople?

By now it is Spring 1097. If you chose to follow Peter the Hermit, you may be dead already! Many of his followers have died from hunger and disease or been killed in ambushes and accidents. Their route ran through Austria, Hungary, and Serbia to Byzantine Empire lands. If you survived that journey, you may have died in a great battle against Seljuk warriors led by Kilij Arslan.

If, instead, you joined armies led by European lords, you might still be alive. In January, you and your comrades ran wild through the streets of Constantinople, capital of the Byzantine Empire, in a disgraceful riot. It was caused by a quarrel over food. You are all starving!

Or Nasty in Nicea?

AFTER MONTHS ON THE MARCH, you Christian soldiers feel mean! You're tired, scared, and suspicious. So when you arrive near the city of Nicea, you just lose control! You attack peaceful farming families, even though they are Christians, set fire to their homes and steal their food. But you quickly forget your shame after winning famous victories. You defeat Kilij Arslan, twice, in May and July 1097.

Or Ambitious in Edessa?

IF YOU CHOOSE to join the troop led by a lord called Baldwin of Boulogne, you will break away from the main Christian army, which is heading south towards Syria. Instead, you will march inland and take over the rich city of Edessa. Watch as Baldwin sets up a new Christian county (or state) there, with himself as ruler, in March 1098!

Handy Hint

Take extra care of your horse! By 1098, four out of every five knights' horses will have died!

I hope it fits. He's become very big-headed lately!

Surround a City and Survive a Siege

It is now October 1097 and if you are still alive you've done very well indeed. Unless you are heading inland to Edessa with Lord Baldwin of Boulogne (see page 23), you will have reached the Holy Land! But as part of the main Christian army, you face a tough time ahead.

You have just arrived outside Antioch, in Syria, one of the most important Muslim cities. Your commanders have set up camp around it and started a siege. They hope to stop all supplies of food and weapons from entering the city. The Muslims trapped inside its walls will either starve to death or be forced to surrender.

At Antioch

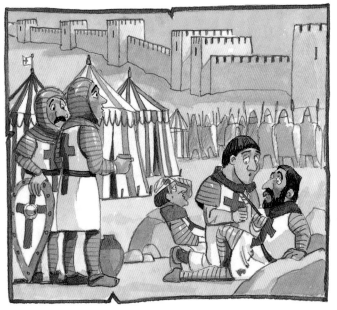

DISASTER! The Turks send an army to attack you and your fellow Christian soldiers. Now you're trapped! For seven months you can't get into Antioch and you can't run away.

SAVED BY A SPY! One of your army commanders (Bohemund) recruits an Armenian spy. He helps 60 Christian knights to break into Antioch. They open the gates and you and your soldiers rush in!

Siege Warfare

ARMORED TUNNELS (left) protect the miners, digging under city walls, from arrows shot by defenders high above.

Put your trust in miracles! At Antioch, a vision of the Holy Lance (spear) inspired soldiers to fight on.

TALL SIEGE TOWERS help soldiers climb over walls, or shoot arrows into the city streets below.

MASSIVE BATTERING RAMS smash holes in walls, gates, and towers.

DEAD, DISEASED BODIES are thrown into enemy cities to spread germs — and fear!

MORE MUSLIM TROOPS arrive and surround Antioch. Now you're trapped inside the city! Conditions are terrible. No food, bad water, and dead bodies everywhere.

YOU ATTACK and the Muslim army rides away! You don't know this, but your victory will be short-lived — another Muslim army is on its way, and then it will be your turn to be besieged.

25

Reaching Jerusalem

Over 60,000 Christians set off from Europe to fight in the Holy Land. Now, in December 1098, only 20,000 are still alive. The surviving soldiers, including you, are starving and shivering in the cold. But you don't turn back. In the spring, when the weather improves, you help lead the Christian army south, to reach Jerusalem. After yet another grueling siege, on July 15th, 1099, you break through the walls around Jerusalem and set foot on holy ground.

Onwards to Jerusalem

TURKEY

MEDITERRANEAN SEA

● Antioch

● Tyre

Jerusalem

JERUSALEM IS OCCUPIED by Muslims from Egypt, who conquered it in 1098. You set up your siege engines and prepare to attack its walls.

BEFORE BESIEGING JERUSALEM, the Christian army walks round and round its walls. This is meant to show sorrow for their sins.

THE CHRISTIAN SOLDIERS are led by bishops and priests, chanting prayers and singing hymns.

THE LAND IS PARCHED around Jerusalem. In the summer heat the Christian troops can't find enough water to drink.

AFTER ENTERING JERUSALEM, horrible events take place. Christian troops massacre all the Muslim men, women and children they can find. The troops also attack Muslim buildings in revenge for the Seljuk damage to Christian ones.

Handy Hint

Don't drink the water! The Muslim defenders of Jerusalem have poisoned wells and streams nearby, to kill attackers.

Will You Ever Return Home?

After helping to capture Jerusalem, what will you do? Will you once again kiss your wife and children and live peacefully in your castle? Only if you are very lucky! Your war lasted for three years, from 1096 to 1099. It was just the first of many Crusades fought in the Middle Ages. In all these wars, many soldiers, just like you, believed they were doing their duty and risked their lives for their faith. Others joined the wars because of greed, ambition, or prejudice.

The Crusades caused tremendous suffering and led to bitterness and misunderstanding between different peoples that still continues today.

What Happens Next?

WILL YOU RISK the dangerous overland journey home, or chance a long voyage back to France by sea? Both are very hazardous – many returning Christian soldiers die this way.

MIGHT YOU STAY in the Holy Land with your victorious war-leaders and help them run a new Christian kingdom, ruled from Jerusalem?

WILL YOU DIE a slow painful death from infected battle injuries? Or perhaps perish in an enemy prison from cold, hunger and thirst?

How Will You Be Remembered?

Handy Hint

Learn from what you've seen! Medieval Muslim peoples have great artistic skills and advanced science, math, medicine, and technology.

AS A CRUSADER? The cross-shaped badge worn by Christian soldiers will give your war —and others like it — a special new name. In about a hundred years from now (around AD 1200) chroniclers will start to call them 'Wars of the Cross' or 'Crusades'.

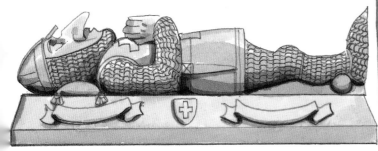

HONORED AS A HERO. Your friends and family think you are a hero for fighting in the Holy Land. So they will pay for a fine tomb when you die. It will be topped with a lifelike carved statue so people will remember you.

REMEMBERED FOR THE WRONG REASONS? Will your name mean only terror to peaceful people in the Holy Land? Will they tell their children sad stories about the suffering caused by the war?

29

Glossary

Ambitious A person who very much wants to succeed or who wants ever more power or money.

Byzantine Empire Formerly the Eastern Roman Empire, ruled by Greeks from the capital of Constantinople (now Istanbul). In the late 11th century it covered most of the Balkans, Greek islands, Cyprus and Turkey.

Caliph Spiritual and political leader of the Sunni (majority) branch of the faith of Islam.

Chain-mail Armor made of hundreds of small metal rings, interlinked then fastened together.

Crusades Wars fought from the 11th to the 16th centuries by European Christians to recapture the Holy Land from the Muslims. There were also Crusades against pagans (non-Christians) in northern Europe, against rebel Christians in France and

Germany, and against Muslims in Spain.

Forgiveness The act of giving a pardon for a wrongdoing.

Gluttony Too great a liking for food.

Grueling Tough, hard and nasty.

Hermit A person who lives apart from the rest of society, usually in a wild, lonely place, to devote himself to God.

Holy Land The land around the holy city of Jerusalem in the Middle East.

Knight Elite, well-trained warrior in

medieval Europe, who fought on horseback, using long spears and heavy swords.

Lance A spear; a sharp metal blade.

Lust A strong desire for something.

Mace A war club, usually with a spiked metal head.

Nomads People without a settled home, who move from place to place to live.

Peasant Farmer who made a living from the land. In the Middle Ages, peasants were bound by law to serve rich, powerful overlords.

Pilgrim A person who goes on a journey to a holy place as part of their religious faith.

Pious To show deep respect for every aspect of a religion.

Pope Leader of the Roman Catholic branch of the Christian Church.

Sea legs The ability to keep your balance and avoid seasickness on board ship.

Sermon A religious speech.

Sloth Too much laziness.

Surcoat A long, loose tunic made of light-weight fabric, worn over a suit of armor to help keep the metal cool in the heat.

Tournament Mock battle fought by knights as training for war and as a court entertainment.

Index

Knight School

Most knights came from the noble class of society, but if you were poor it was still possible to progress through the ranks and become a knight. There were even a few orders of female knights.

Training as a knight began at a young age, when the son of a knight or nobleman would be employed as a page at a lord's castle. Here, he learned skills such as swordsmanship and horse riding.

By the age of 14, the page would advance to become a knight's squire. As a squire, he continued to train with various weapons and learned the chivalric codes of conduct. He was taught the stories of famous, mythical knights such as Arthur and Lancelot, so that he had role models to copy. In exchange for his education, the squire assisted his knight, polishing his armor and helping to clean out his stables.

By the age of 21, a squire was ready to go through the dubbing ceremony and become a knight. He had to spend the night before the ceremony praying alone in a church. At the ceremony, he received an openhanded blow to the neck. He was instructed to behave loyally and bravely in his role as a knight. In reward, he was told to expect a place in heaven.

Did You Know?

Tension

The 11th century AD was a turbulent time for Christianity. The biggest crisis is known today as the East–West Schism (split) or the Schism of 1054. At this time there was a lot of tension between the Eastern Christian churches, based in Constantinople and led by the Greek Orthodox leader Michael Cerularius, and the Western Church, led by Pope Leo IX.

Struggle for Power

Arguments and power struggles in the East weakened the Eastern churches, while the peace in the West allowed the Western Church and its leader to begin insisting on their superior importance. The following struggle for power and control eventually led Pope Leo IX to excommunicate (expel) Michael Cerularius and his followers. Cerularius responded by excommunicating the Pope!

At that moment, the threatened schism between the two churches became a reality. The split between the two churches remains to this day.

A Joint Crusade?

When Pope Urban II took control of the Western Church in 1088, he tried to heal the split. He believed that all of Christendom should be unified. He thought that launching a crusade against the Muslims would strengthen the Christian community and help reunite the Eastern and Western churches. But the Eastern Church never really responded to his call for a joint crusade.